CHANGING YOUR LIFE IN JUST TEN DAYS

CREATING THE LIFE YOU WERE ALWAYS MEANT TO LIVE

MARIE WHITE

SELF-HELP / Communication & Social Skills

PSYCHOLOGY / Mental Health

Special discounts are available on quantity purchases by corporations, associations and others.
For details contact the author.

ZAMIZ PRESS

DO YOU HAVE A MESSAGE TO SHARE WITH THE WORLD? ARE YOU INTERESTED IN HAVING YOUR BOOK PUBLISHED? VISIT ZAMIZPRESS.COM

No part of this publication may be reproduced, distributed or transmitted in any form or by any means, including photocopying, recording, or other electronic or mechanical methods, without the prior written permission of the publisher, except in the case of brief quotations embodied in critical reviews and certain other noncommercial uses permitted by copyright law.

Copyright © 2023 Marie White All rights reserved.

Changing Your Life in Just Ten Days: Creating the Life You Were Always Meant to Live/ Marie White— 4th Ed. Rev. 01/23

ISBN: 978-1-949813-28-9

CONTENTS

Introduction	vii
1. Perspective	1
2. Prepare for the Best	7
3. Chase After Failure	13
4. Build Your Spiritual Life	17
5. Change Your Stinkin' Thinkin'	21
6. Unlocking Your Potential	27
7. Buying Confidence	31
8. Laughter Is The Answer	35
9. Connecting With The People Around You	39
10. Running the Race Ahead	43
11. Continue the Journey	47
About the Author	49

Dedicated to my children.
You make me want to model a life well-lived.
I love you.

INTRODUCTION

Are you living the life you've always dreamed of?
I'll bet your answer is no.

Maybe you've never thought about why your life is the way it is. Maybe you have, but weren't sure how to change it. The following chapters will walk you through ten days of simple steps that will help you create the life that you've always wanted.

Who am I to tell you this? As a mother, wife, TEDx speaker, and the director of publishing for Zamiz Press, I am living a life beyond what I ever could have dreamed. I am the author of several books including *Strength for Parents of Missing Children, Ten Day Bible Study* and *I Think of You*, I also host the popular YouTube channel *Bible Stories for Adults*.

I know that if I can succeed in the midst of hardship, then you can have success as well. It all begins with identifying your goals and going after them.

Your journey to success starts now.

Every strategy I'm going to share with you has been tried by others and I know that each one works. While success doesn't come overnight, if you don't take the first step, you'll never make it to any destination.

You've already taken that first step and if you commit to reading each day individually and completing the exercises that are outlined in each chapter, you will start to change your life.

By this time next week your view of the world could be very different and you could look different too.

Are you ready to begin?

CHAPTER 1
PERSPECTIVE

The first step in changing your life quickly is to gain a better perspective. Let's begin by writing down some key points.

What are the five most important things in your life at the moment?

1. _____
2. _____
3. _____
4. _____
5. _____

My list might look like this:

1. My relationship with God
2. My husband and children
3. Making a difference in people's lives
4. My health
5. Being productive in my work

Those five things determine everything else that I do in life. If I want to do something and it doesn't help one of those five things, then it probably isn't going to happen.

Look at your list.

Every decision you make should be measured by how it affects those five things.

Do you have any goals? Zig Ziglar said that "people can't hit a goal that they don't have."

What are the five most important goals you want to achieve?

1. _____
2. _____
3. _____
4. _____
5. _____

Let's start by looking at number one. Write down three things that are standing in the way of that goal right now.

1.
    A.
    B.
    C.

Move on to your next goal until all five of your goals and the obstacles to achieving them are clearly identified.

2.
    A.
    B.
    C.

3.
    A.
    B.
    C.

4.

    A.

    B.

    C.

5.

    A.

    B.

    C.

Writing everything down does take some work, but that small step will have a huge impact on your ability to reach your goals.

Today's assignment is to listen to this recording about goals. Head to DailyMotion.com or YouTube and do a search for "Earl Nightingale Using Time Management" and click on the 11 minute video.

Sleep on that information tonight and allow your mind to work on the problem. Instinctively your brain will begin to formulate ways to break your goals into manageable pieces. You will start to see paths around obstacles in your way.

Tomorrow we will look at the next step in changing your life.

How does this assignment encourage you or make you feel anxious?

_____
_____
_____
_____
_____
_____
_____
_____

Today's objectives are to:

- Define your goals
- Identify obstacles
- Listen to solutions
- Sleep on problems

CHAPTER 2
PREPARE FOR THE BEST

Yesterday's task was to list the obstacles in the way to achieving your goals. If one of those obstacles was money, then let's delve deeper into the saying "time is money."

When I first started writing, one publishing company offered me a contract and said that if I signed with their company, I would have access to the finest marketing team available.

However, I would be required to find my own monthly speaking engagements, I would have to find my own networking opportunities and I would be required to pay for my own advertising. The way I would pay for their marketing expertise was by giving them a portion of my book's profits, but I would still have to do the actual work.

As a new author I was confused. Wasn't the beauty of a publishing contract that they would do all the work and I would sit back and enjoy the money?

That wasn't how publishing worked anymore.

I knew that many successful people published books on how to market a book. I was willing to use my time and effort to learn and do what that publisher could do— at almost no cost.

My time was actually worth money.

Your time is worth money too. When you don't have the money to spend, learn to do it yourself. You may find that you can do a better job than some of the professionals.

Go back to your list from yesterday.

Highlight the obstacles that involve money.

Think about some ways to accomplish those goals without spending a lot of money.

_____

_____

_____

_____

. . .

If your goal is to go back to school, search online to see which types of college scholarships apply to you. Some scholarships are for single mothers, some are for people over 60 and many for those with incomes under a certain amount of money. Look for special scholarships or student loans that are particular to your state or county. Call the local community college or university and talk to a counselor.

A friend of mine was enrolling her daughter in one course at her local community college and the counselor asked why she was only taking a single class. My friend admitted to the counselor that her daughter had missed the scholarship deadline for that year. The woman informed her that there was another scholarship available right away and it turned out that she could enroll her daughter full-time for free!

The saying is true, "You won't know, if you don't ask."

Attitude is everything.

Attitude can turn defeat into victory, if you learn something from the experience.

There are many things that you can do today to achieve your goals. The first thing you can do is dress for the job that you want. If you want a management position, then start to present yourself as management. Care about the way that you look. Comb your hair, brush your teeth, use deodorant, iron your clothing, show up early, stay a little late and show your employer that you are worthy of a promotion.

If you want to be something more than you currently are, surround yourself with leadership and self-improvement materials.

Not only will you instantly become a more interesting person, but you will begin to understand the job you are working toward.

- If your interest is in trading stocks, then you should have a subscription to the *Wall Street Journal* or read it in your local library.
- If your interest is in botany, then you should have botany magazines and books littering your home.

Saying that you want to start a business, yet not educating yourself on how to start a business and other aspects of entrepreneurship, demonstrates a lack of commitment. You need to eat, sleep and breathe what you say you want to be.

Network with the people around you.

If your goal is to be a reporter, then find out if anyone you know has a friend at the local newspaper or tv station. When you meet someone who is a reporter, ask them how they got started and any tips they might have for entering the business.

People treat you the way you look.

Most of all, people will treat you the way you appear. If you look like a soccer mom, they will treat you like a soccer mom. If you look like a couch potato, they will treat you like a lazy person. And if you are clean, neat and have a confident appearance, people will treat you like a person worth talking to.

Today's assignment is to go to YouTube and look up "7 Steps to Achieving Your Goals Zig Ziglar" and watch the 3 minute 45 second video from the Ziglar Inc. channel.

To get more ideas read this online article in The Huffington Post, search for "52 Tips for Happiness, Health and a Better Life Huff Post."

How does this assignment encourage you?

_____
_____
_____
_____
_____
_____
_____
_____

Today's objectives are to:

- Dress for the job you want
- Get information about what you want
- Find resources in your area
- Network and build relationships

CHAPTER 3
CHASE AFTER FAILURE

Most of us are afraid to make fools of ourselves. In his book *Failing Forward*, John Maxwell says we must embrace failure as a learning experience. His book describes many successful people and the massive failures that launched them into success.

Today's assignment is to listen to this talk from John Maxwell. Go to YouTube and search for "Minute With Maxwell: Possibilities Don't End at Failure" and click on the 2 minute video.

So far this book has introduced you to three amazing motivational speakers, Earl Nightingale, Zig Ziglar and John Maxwell. These men have books and videos that will motivate you for days. If you want to succeed, start listening and reading more from these three.

As it turns out, you don't have to completely revamp your life overnight. All you really need is to identify your bad habits, work to eliminate them, and develop good habits that will help you reach your goals.

I found that if I spent a few minutes each day writing, in a short amount of time I had a book. I found that if I spent a few minutes reading each day, I had read an entire book. And if I spent a few minutes exercising each day, I became fit. It was all about developing new habits and none of them were radical.

A good place to get your reading done is in the car or in the bathroom. Place a book, magazine or article in the bathroom and inevitably the time will come when you have nothing better to do than read. In a few days or months, you will have read it. Mission accomplished.

In the book, *Cheaper by the Dozen*, the family painted the Morse Code on their bathroom wall and by the end of the summer they had memorized it. The same can be done with maps, sign language or Bible verses.

Get rid of distractions, especially apps.

Nothing will waste your time faster, and cause more harm than using phones, tablets and TV to devour the only productive years you have. If these items are addictions for you then tell yourself, "I can watch and play these endlessly—when I'm in a nursing home."

Until then, delete them from your phone, cancel your subscriptions and put time limits on your devices (it's under "settings.")

The book *The Power of Habit*, helps us understand the power of the things that we do on a daily basis. Simple things can take over our time and our lives.

Today's second assignment is to listen to this review from Thomas Frank. Go to YouTube and search for "5 Lessons from "The Power of Habit" by Charles Duhigg" and click on the 5 minute video.

How does this assignment encourage you?

_____
_____
_____
_____
_____
_____
_____
_____

Today's objectives are to:

- Identify bad habits
- Choose good habits
- Initiate bathroom learning
- Remove time sucking apps

CHAPTER 4
BUILD YOUR SPIRITUAL LIFE

Every person has been made for a purpose. Knowing what your purpose is will allow you to focus your energy on that purpose and accomplish a myriad of projects.

John Maxwell paraphrased Mark Twain when he said, "There are two great days in a person's life: the day you were born and the day you discover why."

It's a true statement. Once I knew that my purpose in life was to share the love of God with others, I could not contain my passion for the subject.

My questions to you are:

- What is your purpose? _____
- _____
- Why do you think God created you? ___
- _____
- Are you living your life with purpose? __
- _____
- Have you ever wanted to know what God designed you for? _____
- _____

Today your task is to find out what special traits you've been given in order to pursue your purpose in life.

Here is a free spiritual gifts assessment that will help you identify some of the ways that God has gifted you. Go visit SpritualGiftsTest.com to see what gifts you have.

Knowing God and keeping Him to yourself is not your goal. Knowing Him and sharing His love with others is the ultimate goal.

Is there a way you can help others?

If you're looking for ways to care for people, you can call a local food bank, homeless shelter, or refugee program. If you go to church, ask about volunteering somewhere within your church.

There is no better way to change your life than to invite God into your life. After that, He will help you impact the lives of others.

My YouTube channel, *Bible Stories for Adults* and my book, *Ten Day Bible Study* are both designed to draw Christians to a deeper level of intimacy with God. *Bible Stories for Adults* goes through the entire Bible in short two to five minutes videos.

How would your life change if you had a better understanding of the Bible?

Would you sound smarter?

Would you understand phrases like, "It was a David and Goliath battle," in a new way?

Would you feel more confident?

How does this assignment encourage you?

_____
_____
_____
_____
_____
_____
_____
_____

Today's objectives are to:

- Find your purpose
- Research ways to help others
- Develop your relationship with God
- Think of ways to impact others

CHAPTER 5
CHANGE YOUR STINKIN' THINKIN'

What separates successful people from unsuccessful people? Is it money or influence, could it be opportunity or connections? Family? Geography? Or, could it be their thinking patterns?

Zig Ziglar noticed that during the 1930s and 40s (the time of the Great Depression,) some people were crushed by the economic climate. But he also saw something remarkable— some people did extremely well.

How is that possible?

Mr. Ziglar's example illustrates that it's not what's going on around a person that determines how they do financially, but what's inside a person.

A hard-working, disciplined person, with a great attitude, is always in demand.

A few years ago John Stossel did a special about the traits that cause people to succeed.

Today's assignment is to listen to this recording about this special trait. Go to YouTube and search for "Delayed Gratification Makes for Better Prepared Children" or "John Stossel marshmallow test" and click on the 5 minute video.

Some of the biggest success stories in our country come from legal immigrants who came to the United States with less than ten dollars in their pockets.

These people carried nothing with them except the desire to succeed and the ability to work hard. Many of them did not even speak English.

If you live in a country where you speak the language and have more than ten dollars, you are far ahead of where they started.

They are rich and successful now.

What's your excuse?

If you are reading this and following the steps, then you are already developing the skills necessary to change your life.

A completely new life is only months away from you!

You are headed in the right direction.

Write out your five-year goals:

Where in the world will you live?

What will your home look like?

Where will you work?

What will *you* look like?

What will the people around you look like?

Hold on to that mental picture.

- Start to plan it when you daydream.
- Pick out the couch for the new house.
- Cut out pictures from magazines and create a collage of the life you want.
- Figure out where you'll sit to look out at the ocean.
- Plan the toast you'll give at a big event.
- Start to live your life as if the dream is in view. Because— it is.

Today's assignment is to go to YouTube and look up "PNTV: How Successful People Think by John C. Maxwell." This is on the Brian Johnson YouTube channel.

Brian Johnson notes:

_____
_____
_____
_____
_____

How does this assignment encourage you?

_____
_____
_____
_____
_____
_____
_____
_____

Today's objectives are to:

- Change your thought patterns
- Envision the future you want
- Review the past four days
- Get excited for tomorrow's challenge

CHAPTER 6
UNLOCKING YOUR POTENTIAL

Maybe you've been reading this and thinking, "That sounds great, but I'm not talented enough to make a change in my life."

Today you'll watch one of my favorite Ted Talks.

Sir Ken Robinson will inspire you to take a look at your life and see if there is a talent in you that has been hidden. Your mission is to uncover the talent that is under the surface.

Many of the most talented people on earth suffer from debilitating illnesses. Some of them are too sick or crippled to get out of bed. Other people are blind, deaf, paralyzed, or deformed. They still write bestselling books by dictating books into their computer from bed. They write inspirational songs. They pray without ceasing for missionaries in other countries. They raise money for the poor, start new business ventures, and innovate— all with their debilitating handicap. It doesn't stop them.

Their suffering has produced in them the ability to focus on the thing they believe they are on earth to accomplish and they go after it with everything they have.

You can do the same.

Today, watch these three talks and as you watch them, think about what they have in common. The first one is by Sir Ken Robinson, the second by inspirational speaker Nic Vujicic and the third by the author of this book.

Visit YouTube and type in "Ken Robinson Do Schools Kill Creativity" and choose the 20 minute video from the TED channel.

After watching that, type in "Overcoming hopelessness Nick Vujicic" and choose the 14 minute video from the TEDx Talks channel.

After those two, type in "Marie White abduction TEDx" and click on the 9 minute video from the TEDx Talks channel.

How does this assignment encourage you?

_____
_____
_____
_____
_____
_____
_____
_____

Today's objectives are to:

- Re-evaluate your problems
- See how your struggles help you
- Be inspired by others
- Tell someone about this book

CHAPTER 7
BUYING CONFIDENCE

What if you could buy confidence? Would you jump at the chance to walk into a room completely sure of yourself?

On Google it says that confidence is "a feeling of self- assurance arising from one's appreciation of one's own abilities or qualities."

If you aren't walking around with confidence, it's probably because you have not recognized all of your abilities or positive qualities.

Today let's take a quiz to help identify your abilities and positive qualities. If you already know your skills and interests, you can skip this and move on to the video after it.

You can search online for "free skills test" or use the one at www.whatcareerisrightforme.com.

Today's video will teach you how to give yourself the gift of confidence. It's a wonderful gift to give yourself and it's easier than you may think. Go to YouTube and type in "Your body language may shape who you are Amy Cuddy" and watch the 21 minute video on the TED channel.

Amy Cuddy notes:

_____
_____
_____
_____
_____
_____
_____
_____
_____
_____
_____
_____
_____
_____
_____

How does this assignment encourage you?

_____
_____
_____
_____
_____
_____
_____
_____

Today's objectives are to:

- Identify your skills
- Practice confidence poses
- Use your poses tomorrow
- Evaluate your current job

CHAPTER 8
LAUGHTER IS THE ANSWER

Depression is no laughing matter, but it should be. Why? Because laughter is the best medicine.

Each time you laugh, you release endorphins (feel good hormones) into your body.

Changing your life is easier when you have the right emotional state. While you need perspective, purpose, and focus, you also need the warm glow of laughter in your soul.

Laughing gives you the same feeling as a hot cup of coffee on a cold day. It warms you from the inside out. Why else do you think funny cat videos are always popular? These videos give people an endorphin rush to start the day and help to transform their attitudes. Tony Robbins would call it the correct emotional priming.

If your life is not where you want it to be, ensure that a daily dose of laughter is part of your routine. Laughter has even been shown to help to alleviate both physical pain and stress.

Today's assignment has two parts. The first is to search on YouTube for the video called "Getting unstuck from depression James MacDonald." Please watch that 59 minute video from the All Things Ministry channel on YouTube. If that ever gets taken down, it is also available in a slightly shorter version from the James MacDonald YouTube channel.

James MacDonald notes:

_____

_____

_____

The second part of the assignment today is to get your daily dose of laughter.

On YouTube, explore videos from Brian Regan, Kevin James, Jim Gaffigan and Tim Hawkins. These are all clean comedians that will give you your daily recommended dosage of vitamin L (laughter).

How does this assignment encourage you?

_____
_____
_____
_____
_____
_____
_____
_____

Today's objectives are to:

- Get unstuck from depression
- Practice laughing
- Realize you are valuable
- Take your vitamin L (laughter)

CHAPTER 9
CONNECTING WITH THE PEOPLE AROUND YOU

No one wants to go through life alone. Luckily you weren't designed for a life of solitude. Study after study has shown that being alone is harmful to your mental state and your physical health.

Go online and type in "Loneliness: Causes, Coping With it, and Getting Help." The first article you see should be from Everyday Help (everydayhelp.com). This short article gives you a better understanding as to why today's chapter is so important.

Being alone is not always on purpose, but it often isn't an accident either. The movie, *The Secret Life of Walter Mitty*, did a great job of illustrating how loneliness can be self-imposed and that a bright new future is often waiting around the corner.

Let's go to YouTube and search for "The Secret Life of Walter Mitty: Extended Trailer." Click the 6 minute video from 20th Century Studios India channel and prepare to be inspired.

How you see yourself and how your body feels can have an impact on how you connect with other people. If you're having a hard time finding ways to meet people, take a class. All cities have free or inexpensive community classes in pottery, art, computer skills, book clubs, music lessons, and exercise. Find something that interests you and jump in.

Through acquiring a new skill, you will become a more interesting person and you will meet new people. Expanding your circle of acquaintances will give you access to people you would not otherwise know. They may end up becoming close friends.

John Maxwell talks about connecting with people in one of his YouTube videos. Head to YouTube and search for "Minute With Maxwell: People are Messy - John Maxwell Team." Watch the less than 2 minute video from the Maxwell Leadership channel.

If you want to improve your health search for

the YouTube video called "Best Treatment for Obesity, Diabetes & Cancer" which is available on the Valuetainment YouTube channel.

How does this assignment encourage you?

_____
_____
_____
_____
_____
_____
_____
_____

Today's objectives are to:

- Think of ways to meet others
- Evaluate your mental state
- Realize you are valuable
- Take your vitamin L (laughter)

CHAPTER 10
RUNNING THE RACE AHEAD

Running the Sahara is a terrific documentary movie. Besides being an incredible story of endurance, it also illustrates the power of persistence and cultural conditioning.

One part that stands out to me is when the runner from Taiwan decides to give up. He isn't a quitter. But he seems conditioned to the government controlling his life and that cultural conditioning makes him unable to see a way of getting into a country whose government doesn't want to let the runners pass through.

This cultural conditioning is also evident when his American teammate faces the same news with the attitude of "we'll run right up to the border and do everything in our power to get into the country."

Watching this scene in the movie is really a study in people's reactions to the situations that they are facing. I won't tell you what happens because I don't want to ruin the surprise and it's a movie worth watching. To view the trailer visit YouTube and search for "Running the Sahara (Trailer)" from the PorchLight Worldwide channel."

In life, persistence makes all the difference.

Hellen Keller once said, "Life is a succession of lessons which must be lived to be understood."

Samuel Johnson commented that, "Few things are impossible to diligence and skill. Great works are performed not by strength, but perseverance."

I hope that you have enjoyed this book and that in the ten days that we've spent together you have found some ways to improve your life.

Bookmarking and rewatching these videos once a week will dramatically change your life.

If you get Zig Ziglar's audiobooks and listen to them on the way to work each day they will radically change your life FOREVER.

Your life can and will change if you are willing to put in the work to change it.

Zig Ziglar often said, "People often say that motivation doesn't last. Well, neither does bathing. That's why we recommend it daily."

If you would like to continue making improvements in the days ahead, go to YouTube and search for "Zig Ziglar Attitude Makes All The Difference" from the Ziglar Inc. channel.

You will also enjoy this classic from Earl Nightingale by searching for "Acres of Diamonds Earl Nightingale" available on the Premier Business Global Consultants YouTube channel.

But don't stop there. You've been introduced to some amazing speakers. Look up more from each of the ones you have enjoyed and continue your learning journey. Who knows, some day I may be reading your book!

How does this assignment encourage you?

_____
_____
_____
_____
_____
_____
_____
_____

Today's objectives are to:

- Schedule time for daily motivation
- Realize your new outlook on life
- Share this book with those who need it
- Go to Ted.com and click "Life Hacks"

CHAPTER 11
CONTINUE THE JOURNEY

RECOMMENDED READING

- *The Survivors Club* by Ben Sherwood
- *Ten Day Bible Study* by Marie White
- *Over the Top* by Zig Ziglar
- *Failing Forward* by John Maxwell
- *Outliers* by Malcolm Gladwell
- *The Purpose Driven Life* by Rick Warren
- *The Prayer of Jabez* by Bruce Wilkinson
- *Atlas Shrugged* by Ayn Rand
- *The Knack* by Norm Brodsky and Bo Burlingham

AUDIOBOOKS

- *The Screwtape Letters* by C.S. Lewis
- *Over the Top* by Zig Ziglar
- *Outliers* by Malcolm Gladwell
- *Goals* by Zig Ziglar
- *The Knack* by Norm Brodsky and Bo Burlingham

ABOUT THE AUTHOR

Marie White is the author of eight books, including the multiple award-winning #1 bestseller *Strength for Parents of Missing Children: Surviving Divorce, Abduction, Runaways and Foster Care*. She is a TEDx speaker and the director of publishing at Zamiz Press. You can find her videos as the host of "Bible Stories for Adults" on YouTube, with well over a million views. She encourages people from all walks of life and experiencing a variety of struggles, to know that there is hope.

Her books include the children's books, *Sophia

Wants to Write a Book and *I Think of You,* as well as the adult books, *Your Author Website*, *Ten Day Bible Study*, and more. Visit MarieWhiteAuthor.com.

www.ingramcontent.com/pod-product-compliance
Lightning Source LLC
Chambersburg PA
CBHW030201100526
44592CB00009B/393